T. N. T.
IT ROCKS THE EARTH

A philosophy for today, tomorrow and thereafter with some practical suggestions as to how to get what you want in life.

BY CLAUDE BRISTOL
Writer and Lecturer
(formerly Vice-President of a well-known
Pacific Coast Investment Banking firm)

&

Bob Choat
(2nd Revised Edition)
America's #1 Mind-Body Transformation Expert
Author of 'Mind Your Own Fitness'

Published by
Optimal Life Seminars

MRS. PAT ALLEN

An outstanding woman—

WHO VALUES IT

"No monetary value can be placed on T. N. T. To have the book in your hands is to feel the detonations. Those who seek to accomplish should read it from cover to cover—foreword and all.
Reread it again and again, then prize it through life as a most valued possession."

Original Copyright 1932

Original Revised Edition Copyright 1933

by Claude M. Bristol

2nd Revised Edition Copyright 2012
by Robert L. Choat

All rights reserved. No part of the 2nd revisions may be used, in part or in whole, without the written permission of the author or the author's representatives. This includes electronically and in print.

First Edition—January 1932

Second Edition—July 1932

Third Edition—March 1933

Fourth Edition---October 1933

2nd Revised Edition---October 2012

ISBN-13: 978-1480160644 (CreateSpace-Assigned)
ISBN-10: 1480160644

Published in the United States

To

R.C.W.
who located T.N.T. in my pocket

To
M.J.E.
Who caused me to find it

To
L.B.E.
Who had me use it

To
E.L.B.
Who added to it

And to

all others who aided me in assembling
my supply of T.N.T., this high
explosive is affectionately dedicated.

FOREWORD

It was that period approaching the end of the second year of the great economic depression when hopefulness had almost vanished from business life, and everyone was overwhelmed with fear, that Mr. Claude M. Bristol, my close business associate of many years standing, astounded me by relating a most amazing experience in having found *"that something"* for which he had been searching many years.

As he revealed the truths which had come to him I, at first, was skeptical, but as he took me along with him, I, too, began to see the light which only stimulated my ambition for further knowledge of the theme of how to live powerfully by adopting that science which relates to the development of the human personality.

I realized that there was a great change for good coming over myself, and sensed the possibilities of what could be done if the members of our own organization put the author's teachings into practice, and forthwith arrangements were made for him to talk to our entire staff. The immediate response of every member of our organization in demanding a copy— followed by the most remarkable transformation of individuals and organization, brought home the positive conviction to me that the message contained in his theme was exactly what the world most needed, and that a great service could be rendered by publishing same for general distribution.

In "T.N.T.—It Rocks the Earth," you are told exactly

how to acquire a wonderful secret, that Power, or whatever you wish to call it, which, when accepted and developed through a process of right thinking, creates a philosophy of life which sweeps away all obstacles and brings that which every human desires: success, happiness and contentment.

If it were not for the fact that I am intimately acquainted with the author I would pause to wonder where he acquired those facts and principles which he sets forth in his story, but suffice to say that I know that he knows what he is talking about, and he clearly outlines a system of mechanics which can be used by every one—irrespective of his or her walk in life.

Do exactly as he says, put his plan into operation— and I also promise you that almost overnight you will be transformed and the things for which you have wished all your life will be yours.

Your fears, trials and tribulations will fade into the mists. The door of yesterday will be closed forever. A grand and glorious feeling will engulf you and you will smile, and when you do, the world will smile with you.

I know it. I believe it and it is so.

FRANK W. CAMP.
~TAP~TAP~TAP~

"There is no doubt in my mind that we will get in life what we desire in the ratio of the earnestness of our purpose in going after it."—J. C. PENNEY.

INTRODUCTION
by Bob Choat

Claude Bristol has brought forth in his works the magic that through believing and taking action we can make our dreams happen. In the years since this booklet was first published in 1932 and his later works, 'TNT: The Power Within You' and 'The Magic of Believing', he has helped countless people. Both books I had read years ago and still go through them to this day. And yes, belief is very important for people to take action towards their dreams. Having my latest book, 'Mind Your Own Fitness' published started as a dream that became reality.

Among them are celebrities, including Phyllis Diller and Liberace. In fact, Miss Diller credited 'The Magic of Believing' for her primary success in show business. She was terrified of going into show business and it was Claude Bristol's work that gave her the courage to do so. YouTube has her many interviews documenting this. In Liberace's case, he was known not to be a reader, with the exception of one book, 'The Magic of Believing.' He read and reread and reread that book until the pages became quite worn.

In *TNT: It Rocks the Earth*, you are going to get the basis of Claude Bristol's words and wisdom. He was already in his 40's when this booklet was published and had conducted many years of investigation into success. This is the book that led his later works and helped unleash the TNT in many people – business people and celebrities alike. I am happy to republish this work and do some slight revising for today's world. That includes taking out certain stories that I felt was not appropriate.

I hope you enjoy this volume and start to believe in yourself, your dreams and take action to make them happen. For, it is the combination of belief and action that creates success, turning dreams into reality. So begin the process.... ***Tap—Tap—Tap***

Author's Note:
(from the 1932 version)

To express the thought in another way: We get out of life exactly what we put into it—nothing more, nothing less. So it is with the message within these pages. You will get out of it in the same ratio which you accept the theme and apply the principles.

Therefore, if you wish to develop and get what you want in life, do not loan or give this book away but make it your constant companion and reread it as frequently as possible. The more often it is reread the more workable become the principles and the clearer the road ahead.

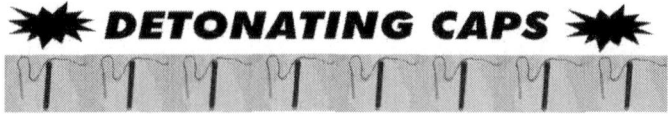

"He who does not know what the world is does not know where he is. And he who does not know for what purpose the world exists, does not know who he is, nor what the world is."
—A FIRST CENTURY MESSAGE

~TAP~TAP~TAP~

For those of you who seek to learn and make progress, I gently lay this in your laps. I do so without the slightest fear but that it will turn your world entirely upside down—bringing you health, wealth, success and happiness, providing you understand and accept.

Do No Misuse It

Remember T.N.T. is a dangerously high explosive so when you gather it closely, handle it gently. Down through the centuries its power has destroyed those who sought to misuse it, therefore **exercise great care that it is used only for good.**

It can be proved by the teachings of the Bible, certain well established laws of physics, and last but not least, just plain common sense. Read and determine for yourself whether or not the proofs I offer stand by themselves.

Some of you may see only the spiritual side, others

recognize the scientific truths, and still others may accept it as just a practical operating device to put you on the road to success. No matter—many know the truth and for you who will open your minds the light will pour in with dazzling white brilliancy.

Feel in Your Pocket

I'm indebted to an old friend of mine, an expert on X-Ray, and electrical high frequency apparatus, who, when I was a boy experimenting with electricity, put the first bit of powerful T.N.T. in my pocket. Then I didn't know what it was and didn't understand, but fortunately it has remained there all through the years. As I look back I realize why he didn't **make** me understand what it was. He believed in me and knew that when I was ready to accept it I would. It's taken nearly 30 years, during which time I sought up and down the highways, looking, seeking and searching for the **SECRET---T.N.T.** All of the time there was some in my pocket—mine for the mere reaching.

However, I've got a firm grip on it now and I will divide it graciously, knowing if used wisely it will blow away all obstacles and straighten out the road on which you've been wanting to travel all your life.

For many years I was a newspaper man and frequently I was behind the scenes. I met great men and women, interviewed famous people. Naturally I studied them and tried to understand what peculiar qualities they possessed that placed them above the others, but their secret evaded me.

Then came the war and I wondered why others made progress while I seemed to be "blocked" in my own ambitions. The war did teach me, however, that I could sleep in the mud, eat moldy bread and live to laugh about it. This is part of my T.N.T. so remember what I learned. It helped me to give old man **FEAR** a solar plexus blow and I believe it will help you.

Hoping to find a royal road to fortune I read hundreds of the so called "**Success**" books and they took me nowhere. I did the same with books on philosophy, psychology and still the great Secret kept just a jump ahead of me. I joined secret fraternal organizations, hoping that I might find that which I sought.

However, just like the bit of T.N.T. in my pocket the Secret was in every book, in the great orders, everywhere, and in fact, right under my very nose but something kept me from it. You will have to determine for yourself what keeps you from it if you don't get it from T.N.T. It's there—if you don't find it in the printed word look between the lines—as I've done my best to present it to you.

Are You Afraid?

Following the war I became a member of a coast-wide investment banking organization and during the years I cherished quite a dream—as did thousands of others in all lines of business—only to discover that the air castles which I built were on an unstable foundation. That something which turned the world upside down financially entirely obliterated my air castles, and I became Afraid. I got lost in the fog. Everywhere I turned something fell in on me. As an executive of the organization my responsibilities multiplied. Our business, due to the economic changes which were taking place in the world, faced a crisis, and many people failing to understand the catastrophe which had overtaken business everywhere were critical. All of which brought worry and many sleepless nights. I found myself dreading to go to my work— fearing that each day would bring added misery.

The weeks went on and conditions got worse and worse. I was baffled. Several times I talked about getting out of the business and one day in the latter part of June, 1931, I made up my mind to leave. 1 mentioned it to one of the women with whom I had been associated for several years and saw nothing but reproach in her eyes. That night I tried to sleep. Again I found it impossible. I paced the floor for hours— when at about 3:30 in the morning I suddenly stopped and sat down. I was face to face with myself. I could follow the inclination to run and leave the others to carry on by themselves, or I could stay and do my share; a duty which I knew was mine. I caught myself saying almost aloud: *"Right is right. It's always been right. It can't be otherwise;"* something I had been taught since infancy.

Suddenly there appeared to be an unfoldment.

Out of the Air

Out of the air came a voice saying: *"What have you been seeking all these years? What were you taught? What did you learn? Where have you been? Where are you going?* I jumped to my feet crying: *"I know it. I've got it now. It's the secret. That's what they tried to teach you. It is the Royal Secret, too."*

Something told me that I would find those identical words in a book which had many years before been given me and which I had tried to read, failed to understand and put aside. It was written by a great man, Albert Pike, a mystic, a poet and a scholar. Grabbing it from the shelf—feverishly I ran through the pages. The words were there and I understood immediately.

Open Your Mind

I now had the key. I could see a broad smooth highway and at the end of that highway a perfect flood of gorgeously beautiful radiance. *"That's the road you are on now. What a simpleton you have been! They tried to teach you, they tried to help you and you kept your mind closed—thinking that you alone could find the road and stay on it."*

I was nearly overcome with the sheer joy of it all. My fears, my worries had disappeared. I smiled. I knew that I was right and that everything would be right for me from then on. I slept like a baby.

There was a different atmosphere in the office that day. The oppressive black clouds which hung over us began to fade away. I told the woman—she with the reproachful eyes—what had happened, and she smiled a knowing smile. She helped me get back on the track and I can never repay her.

As one learned man said: *"All of us are born with the ability to differentiate between right and wrong, and with the ability to achieve, but some of us must run head-on into a stone wall, smash ourselves to bits before we really know what it's all about."* I hit the wall with a terrific crash and it was the greatest and finest thing that ever happened to me.

Many noting the transformation asked for an explanation. I told some of my closest friends. Knowing it will help I give it to all of you.

---Tap---Tap---Tap---

---Tap---Tap---Tap---

Since I caught this theme the book has been put to use by thousands of individuals, firms and organizations. In addition I have talked and lectured, in person and over the radio, to many additional thousands and I am very happy to say that, without exception, phenomenal results have been obtained by those who have understood and applied the principles and mechanics outline herein.

---Tap---Tap---Tap---

---Tap---Tap---Tap---

The morale of our whole organization was at its lowest ebb. Everyone was discouraged. Afraid. By the very necessity of things we had to do an about-face.

Right Is Right

My job was doing everything I could to help the other fellow because I knew it was right. At first I was perplexed as to the methods I should employ to help them, but I used my own system in calling upon the subconscious, and the inner voice said that I should talk to them.

Some were skeptical, but I said to myself; "I can prove that I am right," and during the week that followed I spent every waking hour reviewing the books that I had studied through the years. Naturally the Bible came first; then followed studies in Yogism, the philosophies of the old Greek and Roman masters and of the later day teachers and students. I again deliberated over the Meditations of Marcus Aurelius Antoninus, Reread Hudson's *Law of Psychic Phenomena,* another book, *"The Gist of It,"* written by a brilliant physician, Haydon Rochester. Again I studied my books on physics, electricity and those on the vibrations of light and discovered that not only was I right, as I knew I would be, but that peculiarly the same general basic principles ran through them all. I reread numerous books on psychology and found the same story everywhere. Subsequently I quoted excerpts, and lo and behold, things began to move.

---*Tap*---*Tap*---*Tap*---

It has occurred to me again and again that all men and women who use this **POWER** are showmen, or to use the words of my newspaper days, headliners—those who hit the front page.

Something causes them to toss away the bushel basket under which they hide their heads and they arise above the commonplace.

Where is Your Niche?

Surely you will agree that they may have the **POWER** to the Nth degree, but if they do not become headliners they never get a niche in the hall of fame. It doesn't follow that they are newspaper publicity seekers, because some of them are very reticent—and by their very reticence are showmen.

Others adopt certain peculiarities or use certain devices to make them stand out from their fellow-men. Some wear an efficacious smile, others scowl—and still others have a certain charm of manner.

Long hair, whiskers and sideburns play their part. Flowing robes and distinctive dress are worn by others. The showmanship of some is evidenced by red neckties, others by spats, affected manners.

Many master the art of oratory, the science of warfare, banking, statesmanship, politics, the arts—but all of them stand out in the full glare of the calcium—headliners.

The number is legion. I mention a few of those of history and today: Desmosthenes, Nero, Julius Caesar, Christopher Columbus, Cleopatra, Balzac, de Maupassant, Sir Isaac Newton, Joan of Arc, Cromwell, Edgar Allen Poe, Benjamin Franklin,

Alexander Hamilton, Bismark, Graham Bell, General Grant, Cecil Rhodes, P. T. Barnum, Clemenceau, Kitchener, Woodrow Wilson, Joffre, Sir Thomas Lipton, Foch, *Mussolini, Winston Churchill, Charles E. Hughes, Lloyd George, Mahatma Gandhi, Ramsey MacDonald, Will Rogers, Douglas Fairbanks, Herbert Hoover, Henry Ford, Lindbergh, Alfred E. Smith, *Lenin and *Hitler. They have been and are found in every walk of life.

[*Publisher's Note: During this period of time, no one knew what was about to happen in Europe regarding Hitler and Mussolini and little did those that lived in 1932 think about communism and Lenin. The purpose of Claude Bristol mentioning them was to emphasize the power of belief and action. It's about unleashing your dream, believing in it and taking action. In today's world regarding great orators we go to the likes of the late President John F. Kennedy, Rev. Martin Luther King, Jr., the late President Ronald Reagan and former President Clinton as examples. Remember, people with passion and belief that take action will rock the world. And it could be positive or negative.]

Gandhi uses this **POWER**, I am sure, and I think he is the greatest headliner of present times. You can find many pictures showing him in the modern civilized garb of man, but today, and for several years he has kept his hair cropped short, worn a loin cloth and a pair of huge spectacles. I have no right to say that Gandhi affected this attire for any particular purpose, but I believe he has done it to focus the world's attention upon himself for India's cause.

We have seen Ely Culbertson, the bridge playing expert, perform. There have been few psychological devices that he hasn't used—he has "something"—and certainly no one can say he is not a headliner.

I make no attempt to explain why those who have this **POWER** are showmen. You'll have to determine that for yourself. But remember---

"A city that is set upon a hill cannot be hid. Neither do men light a candle and place it under a bushel..."

Again---

"The great truths of life become known only to those who are prepared to accept them."

I repeat. Thousands who used the POWER for evil brought on their own destruction. We get no less. When we put in good thoughts, constructive efforts and do good then we receive like in return, for---

"Whatsoever a man soweth, that shall he also reap."

Detonating Caps are now set! Caution signals are out. **Be Careful!**

 **IT ROCKS THE EARTH!**

"A man's true greatness lies in the consciousness of an honest purpose in life, founded on a just estimate of himself and everything else, on frequent self-examinations, and a steady obedience to the rule which he knows to be right, without troubling himself about what others may think or say, or whether they do or do not do that which he thinks and says and does."
—MARCUS AURBLIUS ANTONINUS.

There are thousands, yes, millions of people seeking the **SECRET**—the key to health, riches, happiness, contentment and a solution of their problems.

Through the ages many men and women had the secret, used the **POWER** and I am positive you can acquire it too if you'll think as you read, accept and apply the ideas contained herein.

What do you want?
Where are you going?

---Tap---Tap---Tap---

An Old Parable
[Publisher's Note: This story replaced the original]

The Chipmunk Who Wasn't Prepared

The chipmunk plays all day in the warm and sunny weather and every day he passes a squirrel who is busy gather acorns and nuts. Each day the chipmunk asks the squirrel to play with him, but the wise squirrel is getting ready for winter when food is no longer available.

The chipmunk tells the squirrel he has plenty of time to do that and goes on with his playtime every day. The chipmunk continues with his play until one day he wakes up and there is snow everywhere. He has no food stored up so he makes his way out to find food and there is very little.

The little squirrel stays warm in his house all winter, while the chipmunk makes his way out in the freezing cold every day, only to find a tiny morsel after hours of searching. The chipmunk has a long cold hungry winter, just the opposite of the squirrel who is snug, warm and has a full stomach.

As you have read the story, there's much to be learned from it. As you read on, you will fully understand why.

Scoffers Do Not Succeed

I am fully cognizant that some will scoff—there have always been scoffers, but scoffers never succeed. They never get any place in life—simply become envious, while the doer or the person who is moving forward has to jump over or go around them. They have nothing but a nuisance value in life. Some of you may dismiss all of this as you have done before—as you always will—but for those of you who are interested, are still willing to learn, I promise you can learn and make progress for yourself.

I take it there isn't an intelligent man or woman who isn't really interested in getting ahead, but I have often wondered if there isn't a negative quality in most of us which precludes us from really starting.

If You Believe It—It's So

There's a saying I thoroughly believe in: "If you believe it, it's so." Simply a cryptic statement or digest of what I give you. All the great teachers, Buddha, Confucius, Mohammed, Jesus and many philosophers taught a great fundamental idea. It is found in all religions, cults, creeds and sects. Everywhere runs the same general theme—the gist of which in my words is—"If you believe it, it's so."

I quote from the Bible: "As a man thinketh in his heart—so is he." *"As a man thinketh in his heart—so is he"—if you believe it, it's so.* Note the similarity? Reduce the whole thing to one word *"faith."* I have heard many, many people say the day of miracles is past, but never in my life have I heard a thinker, a student or a believer make such a declaration. Surely, the days of Aladdin and his lamp are gone—perhaps they never existed—so with the magic wand, the magic carpet, and all of those things of fairy tale and legend.

Believe in Yourself

When I refer to miracles, I mean those things which can be accomplished through **FAITH**. **FAITH in your belief**; **FAITH in Yourself**; **FAITH** in the persons with whom you are associated. **FAITH** in a

POWER. **FAITH** in **THAT SOMETHING** which controls the destinies of everyone—and, if you can get that **FAITH** and dissipate the negative side, nothing in this world can stop you from acquiring what you desire. While this may sound facetious, there is nothing you can not have if you want it.

Why the Alibis?

All of us are prone to calculate and weigh things, permitting the negative side to creep to the fore, and our thoughts evidence themselves in such remarks as *"It can't be done;" "I'm afraid;" "What will happen if I do it?" "People won't understand;" "It isn't worth the effort;" "I haven't the time"* and similar verbal alibis. If you haven't expressed these thoughts to yourself, then others have to you, and, through the power of suggestion, you have accepted them as your own conclusions.

This same message has been written and delivered thousands of times. It runs through the Bible; you find it in the great fraternal orders; it led the three wise men; the crusaders carried it; every outstanding character of history has used it; Moses, Alexander the Great, Napoleon, Shakespeare, Washington, Lincoln, Roosevelt, Wilson, Benjamin Franklin, Edison, Dr. Steinmetz, Barnum, and thousands of others had a grasp of that something.

The Wise Men Knew

The wise men of all ages, the "*medicine men,*" religious leaders, great teachers, the yogis, the "*healers,*" the "*miracle men*"—all of them knew this secret. Some worked it one way—some another.

They were just human beings. If they knew and could achieve, so can you.

Halt! Think! Ponder! What made Mussolini?

What is it that Aimee has? Gypsy Smith? Billy Sunday? **BELIEF, FAITH**—only that, and the ability of a staunch believer to pass it on to the other fellow. It's the very keynote of all great religions. All big things are started by one person, one believer. It makes no difference where they got the idea originally. All great inventions are the outgrowth of the whole scheme—**FAITH, FAITH—BELIEF** in yourself, your ideas. All super-salesmen know this—they use the **POWER**—that's why they are super-salesmen. Every community drive, every forward movement, everything worthwhile succeeds because some one person has **FAITH** and is able to pass it on and on and on. Think about that—then think about it some more, and think of it again. Meditate over it, and you'll realize that every word is true.

Don't Envy: Do

Many envy the man or woman getting ahead, who appears to be a financial success, a power, an influence. Did you ever seek the explanation? Everything that anyone has ever done constructively has been done from within himself.

Every one of us, if put on the right track, can accomplish what he or she is after by keeping before him or her my own expression: *"If you believe, it's so,"* and adopting the old adage: *"Where there's a will there's a way"* In other words, get that will power—that **FAITH**—that **BELIEF** working every minute of the day—24 hours of the day—7 days a week—365 days a year. And I promise you if it's done you will leave people around you in the progress you make as rapidly as high frequency electrical discharges oscillate through the ether.

Stop! Think! Meditate!

Pause and think for a moment. What is organized propaganda? Nothing more, nothing less than a well developed plan to make you believe. You saw it work in the war days and if you're wide awake to what is going on around you, you know that it's being worked in every line of human endeavor today—just as it was worked thousands of years ago and as it always works. If you're reading the newspaper, listening to the radio and will keep in mind my theme, you will realize that all these speeches of our leaders, our great men coming to us with clock-like regularity are being given with a purpose—to make us believe. Those men know it works.

The Voice Speaks

Mahatma Gandhi upon arriving in England to seek a solution of India's problems said: *"I'm doing this because a voice within me speaks."*

Gandhi referred to *"something"* from within. Call it a **POWER,** call it something supernatural, call it anything you wish. Some refer to it as the subjective mind. Others call it the subconscious mind. Some instinct. Still others to the impulses coming from within as hunches. Divine messages. Spiritualists refer to it as a voice from beyond. No matter what it is, it gets results, and now I show you how to acquire it.

Tap No. 1

First, however, permit me to set the stage by calling attention to the effect of repetition or reiteration. For example, take a pneumatic chisel—you have seen one used in breaking up solid concrete or piercing holes through steel. It's the tap, tap, tap, tap of that chisel with a terrific force behind which causes disintegration of the particles and makes a dent or hole in the object on which it is used.

All of us have heard of the old torture system of dripping water on the forehead. Perhaps you are familiar with Kipling's *"Boots."* It's the tramp, tramp of boots, boots, that makes men mad. It's the constant never-ending repetition that penetrates.

You are familiar with the first part of the picture and how repetition works on material things, but some of you may not thoroughly understand the second part, but here, too, it's the repetition that ultimately makes its impression upon the human mind.

The fundamental of advertising is its repetition, its appeal by reiteration—*"It floats;" "There's a reason;"*

"I'd walk a mile;" "They're kind to your throat." A hundred others all impressed on your mind by constant repetition—tap, tap, tap. Today our leaders are saying the same thing to us though perhaps in a different way. *"Have faith;" "Have courage;" "Move forward;" "Business is coming back"* etc. Repetition, reiteration—again and again. Tap, tap, tap.

The connection between the conscious and the subconscious or subjective mind is close. Every student of the subject knows what may be accomplished by definitely contacting the subconscious. If you can get a definite detailed picture in your conscious mind by using this process of reiteration or repetition and make the subconscious mind click, you have at your command a **POWER** that astounds.

The Science of Suggestion

We hear much about the power of suggestion. We know how easy it is to make a person ill by constantly suggesting to him that he doesn't look well, etc. It's the constant mental review of his crime that suggestion makes a lawbreaker confess. As a newspaper man I have been in on many *"third degree"* sessions.

I have seen detectives and prosecutors corner a single individual and shoot questions at that individual until his face was bathed in perspiration. It is the deadly repetition, the reiteration, the tap, tap, tap, through the power of suggestion which brings confession.

Skilled prosecutors, clever defenders appeal to the emotions of jurors, never to the conscious reason. And how do they do it? Simply by a process of repeating and emphasizing time after time the points they wish to stress. They do it with usage of words and variations of argument. Behind all there is that tap, tap, tap, tap—tapping—the subconscious—making the jurors believe.

If you will keep this idea of repetition in mind you will understand why the Jewish people are so successful in business. When families are gathered together, the subject of conversation is business, business. They talk their problems over—they keep before them constantly the idea of making money and making progress and never for a moment are they permitted to forget. And they stick together.

The idea there was born of necessity, just like a machine or an article is born of necessity. We are all familiar with the old adage, *"Necessity is the mother of invention"*—and it is true of all human impulses and endeavors. A drowning man grabs at a straw. A starving man at a crust of bread.
The impulses come when you get up against it. You who have been there know what you had to rely on in times of acute pressure, and whether or not you heard a little voice from within.

Where Are You Going?

There can be no gainsaying that once you have made up your mind to do a thing it will be done, but the trouble with most of us is that we sidestep, vacillate, and seldom make up our minds to what we want or determine clearly the road on which we wish to travel. All daydreams and wishes would become realities if we kept them constantly before us—put fear behind—shoved away all reservations, ifs, ands and buts. Again, a lot of us think we know what we want when, as a matter of fact, we don't. This sounds paradoxical but, if each of us knew what he wanted, he would get it, provided he had the will-power, the stamina, the dynamic force, the fight to go after it.

Therefore, the first thing to do is get that spirit of determination. That may be obtained by constantly saying to yourself—*"I will" "I will" "I will"* and *"I will"* and believe it. Then before you know it you will have developed a willpower which, coupled with these other things I am about to explain, will change your whole scheme of things and get **You** on the road to success. If you haven't the desire to improve your own individual position in life, then you had better stop reading right now and burn this. However, if you have the desire, you are on your way to make progress.

What Do You Want?

No matter whether you be a salesman, an executive, a mechanic, a writer or what, or whether you are after money, love, improvement in social position, in the legal profession or medical profession, it makes absolutely no difference. You can utilize this power and acquire every single thing you want— whether it be a pair of shoes or a mansion.

Tap No. 2

Now if you have the desire, the foundation is laid. Get a perfect detailed picture of the exact thing, or things, you wish. If it is increased sales, fix the exact amounts; if it's something you want the other fellow to do for you, the love of a woman or the love of a man, a new suit of clothes or a new automobile—anything and everything. No matter what you are after under this system you can have it **provided the desire is definite and positive.**

"He who knows how to plant, shall not have his plant uprooted; He who knows how hold a thing, shall not have it taken away."
-Lao-tzu, The Chinese Mystic, 600 B.C.

Adopt This Tap System

When you have the picture firmly in mind begin using the tap, tap system as I have outlined. It is going to be the repetition, the reiteration of that picture upon the subconscious mind that will cause the little voice from within to speak and point out to you accurately and scientifically how you are to proceed to get what you want. And when you move all obstacles will become phantoms.

Use Small Cards

The idea is to keep the picture or pictures before you constantly. As an aid in the visualization of the things you want and to keep them uppermost in your mind, write a word picture of them on several small cards. (Election card size is convenient). Keep them always in your possession and look at them as frequently as possible—bearing in mind the more often you glance at them the firmer becomes the impression upon your consciousness. As a suggestion, pin one card above the mirror to be looked at in the morning when you shave. Permit the details of your wishes outlined on the card to increase as you continue to develop the mental picture. Have another card convenient to look at while you eat your lunch—your dinner. Use the cards again just before you go to sleep. Keep it up.

Tap, tap, tap. However, there's no point to writing down your wishes until you have determined that every single detail of what you want is to be photographed permanently in your mind—to stay there until they become realities.

[Publisher's Note: You can use 5x8 index cards in writing down your word picture. Also, the use of a dream board in addition to using the cards is appropriate. And like Claude Bristol mentions, make sure that you have every single detail before using the cards or creating the dream board. Actor Jim Carey said this on the Oprah Winfrey Show in 1997: "I wrote myself a check for ten million dollars for acting services rendered and dated it Thanksgiving 1995. I put it in my wallet and it deteriorated. And then, just before Thanksgiving 1995, I found out I was going to make ten million dollars for Dumb & Dumber. I put that check in the casket with my father because it was our dream together." In a sense, the check is much the same as the index card idea.]

Where Is Your Mirror?

Augment the foregoing formula with the use of a mirror. Study yourself in the glass. Search deeply into your eyes. Become acquainted with yourself—know yourself thoroughly and have yourself tell yourself what you want and where you are going. Sooner or later you will see the reflections of your wishes in your mirror every time you peer into it—and your day dreams will gradually take shape. When you get the pictures clearly defined do not for an instant permit them to escape you. Hold them with bands of steel.

"So use all that is called Fortune. Most men gamble with her, and gain all, and lose all, as her wheels roll. But do thou leave as unlawful these winnings and deal with Cause and Effect, the chancellors of God. In the Will work and acquire, and thou hast chained the wheels of Chance, and shall sit hereafter out of fear of her rotations." —EMERSON'S SELF RELIANCE.

Constant practice of writing down your wishes and using a mirror will work wonders. Shortly you can form the pictures at will—without the use of either cards or mirrors—and you will find yourself tapping the subconscious mind almost automatically.

Start Wishing

Don't be afraid of over-doing, or becoming extravagant with your wishes and desires because, as I said before, you can have every single thing you wish, but you must become adept at doing exactly as I tell you. Bear in mind that this whole theme is as old as the universe. The only thing I do is to give you what may be considered the practical mechanics.

As we all know, *"the proof of the pudding is in the eating,"* and if you have any doubts as to whether or not I am giving you an exact science, try it. The automobile will begin to take shape, you will get the new shoes and the bricks of the mansion will fall into place as though a magical hand has touched them.

I know it, I believe it and it's so.

I take it that most of us have been taught the efficacy of prayer. Think a moment. It's the wish—the prayer—with that reiteration, repetition, tap, tap, tap. Keep in mind that, as I said before, you are appealing to the subconscious—to that all powerful force behind—that omnipotent power—a supreme intelligence—or whatever you wish to call it.

The Ancients Tapped

It is easier to go with the current than fight against it, but you must harmonize with others, with everything around you.

"No longer let thy breathing only act in concert with the air which surrounds thee, but let thy intelligence also now be in harmony with the intelligence which embraces all things." — THE WORDS OF A GREAT PHILOSOPHER.

It shouldn't be necessary for me to explain that I am suggesting that you put yourself in tune with the very stream of life itself. You who understand will appreciate that nature provides ways and means for all things to grow rightly. Meditate for a moment and you'll realize I am giving truths which many may have forgotten. There's the great fundamental law of compensation which makes all things right.

There's no set rule for doing anything because some of us perform one way and some another, just as two people go across the river—one goes by one bridge and one another—but they both ultimately get to their destination. In other words, after all is said and done, it's results that count, and, if you will make up your mind to exactly what you want and follow the simple rules which are given herein, everything you are after will be yours.

I know it, I believe it and it's so.

After you get a grip on the Power do not let the results of its usage surprise you. Miracles will be performed. You will do what previously you thought impossible.

Tell No One

It is not well that you should tell anyone of your wishes or desires — your innermost ambitions. Keep them to yourself, for should some persons learn what you are after they may place obstacles in your way and otherwise attempt to hinder you. Should barriers accidentally fall or be placed in your path, climb over or go around them. Go whistling blithely by. Remember nothing can stop you but yourself.

I know it, I believe it and it's so.

I also am one of those who believe that all things are relative. To my way of thinking if a man can earn one dollar he can as easily earn ten. If he has two suits of clothes—he can have ten. The only difference is the amount of energy he is willing to expend and this goes for acquiring $100 to $1000 and from then on it is a matter of only adding ciphers. There is no limit as to what a person may do or secure provided he makes up his mind and steadfastly and determinedly moves towards his goal.

"Look within. Within is the fountain of good, and it will ever bubble up, if thou wilt ever dig" —AN ANCIENT SAYING.

Use It Only For Good

As I said under Detonating Caps be careful how you use the Power which is to be yours. It will act as a boomerang and destroy you and everything you hold dear if you use it for evil. Therefore only use it for doing you and others the most Good and bringing Happiness for yourself and those around you.
Do not talk or boast about what you may have done for others or of your good deeds. They will speak for themselves. Just continue to give thanks for the fact that you are on your way— that's enough.

Have You Got It?

What is personality? What is it that, when you get in the presence of another person who has personality, that grips you? What is it that causes you to feel his very presence—that overshadows you? It's nothing more than a dynamic force coupled with will power which is drawing from that huge reservoir of the subconscious. There are millions of people who have this personality—some say it's natural with them—perhaps it is—but they are unconsciously using this **Power.** In other words, it's sort of been thrust upon them and when that thing called personality is backed up with will power, things move. To my way of thinking selling bonds, books, clothes, insurance, electric service, washing machines, is no different than selling any other commodity—selling yourself or selling ideas. I have found that trying to put over an idea, firstly I have had to believe in the idea—dream it, eat with it, sleep with it—I had to have it with me every minute of the day until it became part of me—the old idea of repetition again—and I know it works in selling commodities. You have got to know what you are talking about and only hard, personal, persistent, intelligent study will enable you to do this.

One more thing, and that is keep informed as to what is going on in the world about you. You never know what a prospect may be interested in and it's sometimes necessary to get his attention for your "break" entirely through irrelevant subjects — that's why I repeat, read the newspapers, current periodicals, and read them thoroughly. I don't mean read every detail of some murder or suicide, but get a digest of the day's news. Awaken, know what is going on about you.

Tap No.3

Keep step with the world's affairs. The better informed a person, the better he is equipped to get what he wants. Don't forget that Knowledge is Power—all of you should know that by this time.

"He who knows others is clever, but he who knows himself is enlightened."
—FROM THE SAYINGS OF A WISE ORIENTAL.

Increase your knowledge and the scope of your activities will be enlarged and the desire for greater things—larger things, will come automatically and, as they do, the things which you previously thought you wanted will become to your mind trivial and will be disregarded, which is another way of saying that you ultimately will hitch your wagon to a star and, when you do, you'll move with lightning-like speed.

Study, learn and work. Develop a keenness of observation. Step on the gas. Become alive for yourself and you'll pass it on to the other fellow. Get confidence, enthusiasm and you'll set up like vibrations all around you and that's the theory of all life—as old as the world itself. Like begets like—a laugh brings a laugh—a good deed calls for a good deed—riches beget riches, love, love— and so on.

The old law of attraction stated in Ampere's theory of electrical magnetism is: *"Parallel currents in the same direction attract one another"*— and when you are out of tune and antagonistic you put others out of tune and make them antagonistic because:

"Parallel currents in opposite directions repel one another."

Wishbones Need Backbones

However, don't get the thought that I have given you an oversize wishbone which will enable you to sit down and, by talking to yourself, through the idea of repetition, get what you want, because it will never work. You have got to have the wishbone backed up with a backbone and that isn't all—the wishbone and the backbone must be coordinated and synchronized to a point where they are running in perfect harmony, and when they are in tune, you will find personality developing.

I take it that all of us have admired that intense type of person. I mean by that, one whose shoulders are back, whose chest is out, whose head is up and whose eyes are alert. It is easy to pick out in any organization those whose feet lag, whose shoulders droop, whose chins sag and whose eyes are a blank. Drifters, loafers, quitters. First measure yourself. Then study those with whom you are associated and you can tell at almost a glance those who will make progress and those doomed to failure.

Every physical movement tells a story—each marks your personality. Take another good look at yourself in the mirror and probe again and again. You know whether you've got it or not. If not, make up your mind to get it—you can and you will if you make up your mind.

The Eyes Have "It"

If you will develop that intensity of purpose, determination to get ahead, shortly that determination will show in your eyes. You have heard people say that a certain person has a penetrating gaze—that he looks right through one. What is it? Nothing more than that fire from within—intensity—or whatever you wish to call it, which means that the person who has that gaze usually gets what he wants. Remember the eyes are the windows of the soul. Look at the photographs of successful men—study their eyes and you will find that every one of them has that intensity; therefore, I say, let it be reflected in the way you walk, in the way you carry yourself and it will not be long before people will feel your presence when you walk through a crowd—and an individual prospect will feel that personality when you talk with him.

All of this is to explain that it takes an affirmative type to make progress and the things I have pointed out may be utilized to develop you into an affirmative type. The negative type is sunk before he starts. Nature takes care of these situations through the old law of the survival of the fittest. We know what happened in the days of Sparta when children were put on their own at a baby age and only those who survived were given further chance. A negative type is a quitter, or, another way, a quitter is a negative type and, while there is no point to going around hitting everybody on the nose just to start something, always remember it's poor business to let yourself be put on the defensive as that is a negative sign. The person who won't be licked, can't be licked. If you are taken unawares and suddenly put on the defensive, snap out of it. Take the offensive because, if you remain on the defensive, you are beaten.

Every Day—in Every Way

Of course, to bring about this intensity of being, it's necessary to be in good health. I do not claim that the power of will is a cure-all to mend broken legs and all that sort of thing, but I do know that constant application of the theory herein advanced will aid a person in ill health. All of you have heard of Dr. Emil Coue, the Frenchman, who was in this country a few years ago, telling people they could cure themselves if they would adopt his plan.

His idea was that you should say to yourself—*"Every day, in every way, I am getting better and better."* Just ponder over that for a minute. There was nothing new in that idea, any more than there is in the ideas which I put forth. Simply another way of expressing the whole scheme—reiteration, repetition—keeping upper-most in your mind all the time what you want and which positive thoughts, in turn, are passed on to the subconscious mind—the wonder thing. Think health, wealth and happiness and they will all be yours. It cannot be otherwise.

We all know of people who are continually talking about backaches, headaches or some other kind of aches. They harp on them and the first thing they know, with that reiteration, the aches become realities. If you have such an ache or pain there is no point to talking about it; neither is there any point to talking about your worries, your troubles. Do not talk about them. Do not think about them. Then they will not be in your mind. It is the repetition that keeps them there. Shift your gears—reverse the process. Get away from the negative side and become an affirmative type—think affirmatively and the first thing you know your aches, worries and troubles will disappear.

"If thou art pained by any external thing, it is not this thing which disturbs thee, but thy own judgment about it. And it is in thy power to wipe out this judgment now. But if anything in thy own disposition gives thee pain, who hinders thee from correcting thy opinion?" —PHILOSOPHY OF THE AGES.

Are You in Reverse?

When a train roars across the track in front of you, you put on the brakes of your automobile, throw the gears into neutral and idle your engine—you are on your way again just as soon as the train passes but you certainly do not throw your gears into reverse and go backwards.

Compare yourself to the gears of your automobile. In reverse place all fears, worries, troubles, aches and pains. And when things go wrong simply put on the brakes, idle your engine until you can clearly see the road ahead. In high is everything you desire, health, wealth, happiness—success. No power in the world except your hand can put the gears of your automobile in reverse. If your own gears get in reverse remember you alone put them there. And you put them there with your own thoughts because:

"There is nothing either good or bad, but thinking makes it so." –Hamlet—Act ii, Sc. 2

Therefore, as you think, you move either forward or backward—in high gear or in reverse. When you place yourself in reverse, worry, stew and fret you are using the tap, tap, tap idea to bring into existence the things you would most avoid.
Some 3500 years ago Job said:

"For the thing which I greatly feared is come upon me, and that which I was afraid of is come unto me."

Certainly they came upon him because he, in his fears pictured them—he used the immutable law to attract them. Just as you bring the good things which you want into reality by holding the positive thoughts constant so do you bring the bad things—those which you fear—by holding the worry, the negative thoughts constant.

Which Will It Be?

If you have read this far then you must realize that when you look after your thoughts—then your thoughts will look after you. Therefore, which will it be—grief, trouble, ill health, worry, failure or health, wealth, happiness—success? It's entirely up to you—no power on this earth but you can direct your thoughts—and the way you use your **WILL** to keep your thoughts positive is a matter solely under your control. Therefore, lose no time in erecting a steel wall on the right side of the reverse gear, close the door of yesterday—keep it closed always—then shift from low gear into high and stay there.

Those of you with your own business, increase your business—or if you're a salesman, your sales—as a result of your own thinking. When others tell you that business is bad, things are tough, going to the bow-wows, etc., and you accept their thoughts and make them your own, your business will go the bow-wows. Have no doubt about that. [Publisher's note: "going to the bow-wows" was a common saying back in the 1930s. In a sense, it means "going to the dogs."] Then as you talk to others, with your chin on your chest, your feet dragging and the front of a professional mourner, then you tap them down and the more you circulate and the more you talk (tap, tap, tapping with the same story) especially, if you think and talk with an air of conviction, the more damage you do. You are setting up *"thought"*—in reality **FEAR**—vibrations which are far reaching. Fear thoughts are terrifically contagious and spread like wild fire. Conversely as you direct your thoughts (visualizing) towards increasing your business, your sales, your profits, etc., have no misgivings of your own (keeping your mind closed to the downward tapping thoughts of others) and put enthusiasm, energy and action into your program, your business, your sales automatically will increase. You must keep in mind always that the intense fire of enthusiasm from within becomes a conflagration which affects all on your wave length as long as you radiate it. The vibrations you set up with your powerful rays of enthusiasm inspire others, raise them up, build and attract business—just as **FEAR** vibrations tap others down, repel and destroy.

It is an indisputable fact, irrespective of the times, that there is always business somewhere for the man who **BELIEVES** it exists and goes after it but none for the person who is positive that none exists and make no endeavor to move.

ACCEPT THIS!

EXPERIMENT, AND BE CONVINCED.

Any downward or upward in our worldwide economic scheme is due entirely to the way we think. When the great world leaders—the statesmen, the financiers, editors, publishers, economists --- those who direct and influence the thoughts of millions in every part of the globe permit depressed thoughts to enter into their scheme, then depressed thoughts and **FEAR** vibrations enter into the scheme of those same millions and business come to a near standstill. When the world's leaders change their way of thinking— toss out **FEAR** and move forward instead of backwards, then the thoughts of millions change for the better and as they think constructively business improves.

Stop and meditate over this for a few moments. You will realize that *"thought"* operating in reverse was the great underlying factor which brought on the so-called economic depression. Human beings are human beings the world over—whether in Prague or Timbuctoo—all subject to the same emotions, the same influences, the same vibrations; and what is a community, a city, a nation but merely a collection of individual humans?

"As a man thinketh in his heart—so he is."

As members of a community think—so they are; as a city thinks—so is it, and as a nation thinks— so is it.

There is no other conclusion.

"We are living in a great crisis in human history. There is unlimited need for boldness and courage, but there is no occasion for dismay. On the one hand there is the way to such achievements, to such wealth and happiness as mankind has never before known.... life, even as we know it now, tastes very good at

times. We spoil it a lot for ourselves and each other by fear, follies, hate, bickering, suspicion and anger. There is no need for us to go on spoiling it. We have not the health we might have. We have not a tithe of the happiness we might have. But it is within the power of the human will to change all that."
—H. G. WELLS. ENGLAND'S GREAT MAN OF LETTERS.

---Tap---Tap---Tap---

Change Gears Now

This power—this vital energy—or whatever it is, is inexhaustible, and it is so easy to use it if you only have the key. I am fully appreciative of the fact that psychologists maintain that few persons really think. It is my hope that this message will cause **You** to Think. If you dismiss it as so much balderdash, then I shall know that you have never understood or appreciated how the great characters of history whom I have previously mentioned and many others with whom you yourself should be familiar made names for themselves or gained niches in the hall of fame.

Real people—successful people, are those who made themselves and not what others made them. After all, there are only two ways to move, forward and backward—why not forward? Watch the down-and-outer on the street. His whole trouble is lack of positive ideas. If he thinks he is down and out—he is. If he will change his ideas, he will be up and coming. All of us know that.

You can shift your gears if you only realize it. You

have been told how to keep out of reverse and it is simply a mechanical process for yourself. Understand and you will always keep your gears in high and move forward.

---Tap---Tap---Tap---

Believe in Your Goods

A sale is affected by getting a prospect to think as you do and, unless you believe that the thing you are selling is good then, obviously, you can't make the other fellow believe it.

That is just plain common sense—so, for those of you who may be selling keep in mind what I have previously said about knowing your article and selling yourself—that is 99% of the success of selling—the other 1% is leg work contacting the prospect.

You should realize that the bending other people to your will or getting them to do as you wish is simply having them think as you think and that is very easy.

Sell Yourself

Charles M. Schwab said: *"Many of us think of salesmen as people traveling around with sample kits. Instead, we are all salesmen, every day of our lives. We are selling our ideas, our plans, our energies, our enthusiasm to those with whom we come in contact."* So it is with every endeavor, and especially true of selling commodities because you must contact people.

And when I say contact, I mean contacting them face to face. The day of order taking is gone and it is only the persons who have got it in them who are to succeed now—all the others will sink. You cannot beat a fundamental law—*"the survival of the fittest."* Therefore, forget about order taking and keep in mind the only way you can close a sale is to make the prospect think as you think—the best way is in face to face contact—you have got to be in his presence—you have got to see his reactions— *"the old law of cause and effect"*—and you have got to adapt yourself to the conditions as they confront you with that individual prospect.

Follow Your Hunches

If you are intent on making a sale—and you must be if you are going to succeed—keep in mind my theme, the subconscious mind will be giving you ideas, hunches, inspirations, a perfect flood of them, which will guide you correctly. They will point out the way to get into a busy man's presence—into the privacy of his very self and, when you get there, stand on both feet.

Be alert. Make him feel your personality. Know what you are talking about. Be enthusiastic. Don't quail.

You are just as good as he is and, besides, you may have something which he hasn't and that is utmost confidence, utmost faith in the article you are selling. On the other hand, if he is a success he also has personality—therefore be sure to put the contact on a fifty-fifty basis. Do not belittle him—do not let him belittle you. Meet on common ground. Make him like you and when he likes you and you him, success is on its way. Remember you are going to sell him.

There is strength in team work. The *esprit de corps* pounded into those of us who were in the army made the American forces what they were—and it's the *esprit de corps,* team work, determination to move forward which will shove us along. If this is accepted in the spirit in which it is given; put into execution, you will be unbeatable. And by getting in tune and getting others on the track, the world is yours.

"When fear rules the will, nothing can be done, but when a man casts fear out of his mind the world becomes his oyster. To lose a bit of money is nothing but to lose hope—to lose nerve and ambition—that is what makes men cripples." —HERBERT N. CASSON.

Ascertain exactly what you want and use the mechanics given and you will discover more gates open for you than you ever dreamed existed. I am not interested in any prophetic explanations—I am interested in results. A light will dawn upon you and you will see clearly ahead how to achieve what you are after. The same principles, the same methods can be successfully applied to any line.

The ability to accomplish anything in a convincing fashion depends entirely upon the degree of expert knowledge which you possess coupled with that intensity of purpose. Read and study, practice, practice, tap, tap, tap.

Open the Door

Before closing I should tell you that the conscious mind must be placed in a receptive condition to get the ideas from the subjective or subconscious. Of course, we all know it is the conscious mind which reasons, which weighs, which calculates—the subconscious mind does not do any of these things—it simply passes on ideas to the conscious mind.

Relax and Tap

You have heard a lot of people say; "play your hunches" — what are those hunches? Where do they come from? They come from the workings of the subconscious mind. Psychologists tell us—you will soon understand the reason—that to put the human mind in a receptive condition you must relax. If you have ever laid on the massage table and been told by the masseur to relax then you know what I mean. Let the body go limp. If you have trouble at first, try it with your arm—both arms—both legs, until the whole body is relaxed and the mind automatically will relax.

When that is accomplished concentrate on what you want—then hunches come. Grab them, execute them as the little voice tells you. Do not reason or argue, but do as you are told and do it immediately.

You will understand what psychologists, mystics and students mean when they tell you to stop, relax— **Think of nothing**— when you wish to draw on the subconscious and have the little inner voice speak. As you further progress you will also begin to realize what the seers of the East had in mind when they said: *"Become at ease, meditate, go into the great silence, continue to meditate and your problems will fade into nothingness."*

The road ahead will become illuminated and your burdens will fall away one by one. Is there anything clearer than "*Pilgrim's Progress*?" My message is no different than that which was conveyed there—only, as I said before—I put it to you in perhaps different words.

The Mysterious Nothingness

The late Thomas A. Edison explaining his success of inventing said: *"I begin by using my accumulated knowledge but most of my inventions are completed with Ideas which flash into my mind out of thin air."*

Fred Ott and Charles Dally, associated with Mr. Edison for more than 50 years, solved the secret of making synthetic rubber. I quote from a newspaper story dated October 21, 1931: *"On Monday, he (Mr. Edison), started to sink into a stupor. But Dally and Ott were still pounding doggedly (determinedly, concentrating, tap, tap, tap) at their experiments. And on Tuesday night the solution flashed out of the mysterious nothingness."*

The little voice spoke—just like it always does when you make up your mind what you want and when you go after it.

If your own little inner voice suggests that you ask for something, do not be backward about asking. You have nothing to fear. The other person will never help unless he knows your wishes so you must ask.

Accept the theory advanced herein and practice intelligently and the voice will speak just like it did for Edison, Ott, Dally and thousands of others, and you will get results—all will be yours.

In Julius Caesar, Cassius, he of the lean and hungry look, talking to Brutus, of the Roman Emperor's power, said:
"The fault, dear Brutus, is not in our stars, but in Ourselves that we are underlings."

As you know, William Shakespeare wrote that, and he himself arose above the commonplace by using this **POWER.**

Who is to Blame?

If you are timid, backward, in a rut and an underling, it is because of yourself. Blame not the stars. Blame not society. Blame not the world. Blame **Yourself.** Again I say, change gears. Put them in **High** and **Begin to Move.**

Grip Tightly

Some people not thoroughly understanding may say that you are conceited, self-centered, or selfish but care not what they say. Those are the scoffers—those who would put rocks in your road and otherwise impede your progress. Those who understand will be helpful—they will be eager to serve you. The intelligent ones will begin to study you to determine what you have that they haven't and try to learn your secret.

I have given you a grip on it; hold it to you tightly and start moving forward.

George Jean Nathan, one of America's foremost critics, in a compilation of *"Living Philosophies"* declares he has never known a man who succeeded in life in a material way who did not think of himself first, last and all the time. Naturally I don't know just how Nathan meant that but I am sure he did not mean that a successful man is selfish to the point where he isn't helpful to others because if you follow the theme as I have outlined it and get on the road to success you will not be led to act ruthlessly.

Service Pays Dividends

As a matter of fact, the exact opposite is true because you will find that you will wish to do charitable things, good things for other people, performing services involving the throwing out of crumbs as it were, and your willingness to do something for the other fellow will bring about a willingness on his part to do something for you. There is nothing selfish about this—it's just a matter of cause and effect.

Remember Ampere's laws of attraction. *Like begets like.* When you perform a service you will be paid huge dividends. There is no mystery about it, it's just so.

---Tap---Tap---Tap---

"I am the master of my fate, I am the captain of my soul."
—HENLEY.

---Tap---Tap---Tap---

"As a man thinketh in his heart—so is he." —JESUS.

---Tap---Tap---Tap---

I know it, I believe it and it's so.

---Tap---Tap---Tap---

T.N.T.—It rocks the earth!

Practice Tap, Tap, Tap

This little book will do everything for you that is claimed buy you must reread it and reread it until every sentence, every word is thoroughly understood and then you must apply the principles and mechanics with your heart and soul. Make them a part of your daily life and when you put into practice the ideas offered you will find that they will work just as they've always worked and always will. If you are in deadly earnest with yourself you will find the whole scheme very simple.

Reread It Reread It Reread It

After you have studied the book and have reflected upon the ideas set forth you will appreciate the tremendous force which lies in the science of thought repetition and positive action. You can, by repetition of the same thought, "tap" yourself upward or downward—dependent on whether you have depressed or constructive thoughts and as you build yourself powerfully you will find that you can influence others by your thoughts. Therefore, let me again admonish you to exercise great care that you do not misuse you **POWER**. Keep your mind filled with good, constructive thoughts and then act with all the energy you possess as the ideas come to you. Remember: Every thought, kept over constant, leads to action and result follow. So keep this book and reread it, study it and reread it and study it as frequently as possible. Practice, tap, tap, tap.

> *In the beginning all things were good. Man, himself, made them bad. You do evil and evil will be done to you. You do good and you will receive good in return. You can be what you wish and have everything you want, provided, you are willing to pay the price in time, thought, effort and energy. You now have the key—may you make it work.*

T.N.T.—It rocks the earth!

T. N. T.—It Rocks the Earth.

Here, there—everywhere.
Wenn Sie es glauben—ist es so.
Si vous le croyez—alors c'est vrai.
Om Man tror det—ar det sa.
Se voi Credete è—co si.
Si creyo is V—es asi.
If you believe it, It is so.

T. N. T.—It Rocks the Earth.

"The more you spread it (your message) the greater will become the service you are rendering to your fellow men." —PAUL R. KELTY, *Editor,* THE OREGONIAN. Portland, OR

Many others, believing that great good must follow, urged me to get my message circulated and this little book is the result. I know what it has done; I know what it will do when passed on to others.

You have friends and acquaintances who are depressed, despondent, in ill health, worried over financial affairs, whose worlds are topsy turvy; dissatisfied with their lot in life — lost in the wilderness. You may perform a great service by having them read T. N. T. and they need never know that you were responsible for their receiving it.

About Claude Bristol

He was born in 1891 and served in the U.S. Army during WW1. During his military days he was a reporter for *Stars and Stripes* until 1919. As a tough journalist during the 1920's, he also had a stint as a large city editor for the church section.

Claude Bristol read many books during this time, including those in psychology, metaphysics, religion and science as well as ancient studies. His knowledge was well-rounded as he was able to deduce the true reason why some people became successful while others fell onto hard times.

How I came to tap the power of belief
by Claude M. Bristol

Is there some force, or factor, or power, or science -- call it what you will -- which a few people understand and use to overcome their difficulties and achieve outstanding success? I firmly believe that there is, and it is my purpose in this book to try to explain it so that you can use it if you desire.

Around 1933 the financial editor of a great Los Angeles newspaper attended lectures I gave to financial men in that dry and read my brochure *T.N.T. -- It Rocks the Earth.* Afterwards, he wrote,

"You have caught from the ether something that has a mystical quality -- a something that explains the magic of coincidence, the mystery of what makes men lucky."

I realized that I had run across something that was practical and workable. But I didn't consider it then (neither do I now) as anything mystical, except in the sense that it is unknown to the majority of people. This "something" has always been known to a fortunate few down the centuries, but for some unknown reason it is still barely understood by the average person.

Years ago, when I started to teach this science by means of lectures and my brochure, I wasn't certain that the concepts could be grasped by the ordinary individual. But since then, I have seen those who have used it to double and triple their incomes, build their own successful businesses, acquire homes of their dreams, and create sizable fortunes. I am now convinced that any intelligent person who is sincere with himself can reach any heights he desires. I had no intention of writing a second book, although many urged me to do so. But a few months ago, a woman in the book business who had sold many copies of my first little book literally read me the riot act:

"You have a duty to give to the men and women who seek places for themselves in the world, in easily understood form, the new material that you have given in your lectures. Everyone of ambition wants to get ahead, and you have amply demonstrated that you have something that will help anyone. It's up to you to pass it along."

It took time to sell myself on the idea. But having served as a soldier in World War I, mostly in France and Germany, and having been active for many years in ex-service men's organizations as well as a state commission for the rehabilitation of ex-service men and women, I realized that it would be hard for many individuals to make outstanding places for themselves in a world from which they had long been separated. It is with a sincere desire to help them, as well as all ambitious men and women, that I write this more full and detailed exposition of **the Power of Belief**. Thus this work is written also to help develop individual thinking and doing.

Since this book may fall into the hands of some who may call me a crackpot or screwball, let me say that I am past the half-century mark and have had many years of hard practical business experience -- as well as a goodly number of years as a newspaper man. I started as a police reporter. Police reporters are trained to get facts and take nothing for granted. For a two-year period I was church editor of a large metropolitan newspaper, during which I came in close contact with clergymen and leaders of all sects and denominations, mind-healers, divine healers, Spiritualists, Christian Scientists, New Thought-ers, Unity leaders, sun and idol worshipers -- and, yes, even a few infidels and pagans.

The well-known English evangelist Gypsy Smith was making a tour of America at that time. Night after night as I sat on his platform, watching people stumble down the aisles, some sobbing, others shouting hysterically, I wondered....

Again I wondered when I accompanied the police in answering a riot call: some Holy Rollers in a moment of hysteria had knocked over a stove and set fire to their meeting hall. When I attended my first (and only) meeting of Shakers, I wondered -- as I did while attending various spiritualistic meetings. I wondered as I heard the testimonials at the Christian Scientists' Wednesday night meetings. I wondered when I watched a group of people immersed in the icy waters of a mountain stream and coming up shouting "Hallelujah!" even though their teeth were chattering. I wondered at the Indians' ceremonial dances and their rain-dance rituals. Billy Sunday also caused me to wonder as, in later years, did **Aimee Semple McPherson**.

In France during the First World War, I marveled at the simple faith of the peasants and the powers of their village *curées.* I heard stories of miracles at Lourdes, and of somewhat similar miracles at other shrines. When in a famous old Roman church, I saw elderly men and women climb literally on their knees up a long flight of stairs to gaze upon a holy urn -- a climb that is no simple task for an athletically trained young person -- I wondered again.

Business brought me into contact with the Mormons, and when I heard the story of Joseph Smith and the revelations on the plates of gold, I was again given to wonder. The Dukhobors of western Canada, who would doff their clothes when provoked, likewise made me wonder. While in Hawaii I heard much about the powers of the kahunas who could, it was claimed, cause people to die or live by praying. The great powers attributed to these kahunas profoundly impressed me.

In my early days as a newspaper man, I saw a famous medium try to make "spirits" respond before a crowded courtroom of antagonistic scoffers. The judge had promised to release the medium if he could get the "spirits" to speak in the courtroom. Yet they failed to materialize, and I wondered why -- because the medium's followers had testified to remarkable séances.

Many years later, I was commissioned to write a series of articles on what the police call the "fortune-telling racket." I visited everyone from gypsy phrenologists to crystal-ball gazers, from astrologers to spiritualistic mediums. I heard what purported to be the voices of old Indian "guides" tell me the past, the present, and the future, and I heard from relatives I never knew existed.

Several times I have been in a hospital room in which people around me died, while others with seemingly worse ailments were up and -- apparently -- fully recovered within a short time. I have known of partially paralyzed people who got over their condition in a matter of days. I have known people who claim to have cured their rheumatism or arthritis by wearing a copper band around their wrists -- others by mental healing. From relatives and close friends I have heard stories of how warts on hands suddenly disappeared. I am familiar with the stories of those who permit rattlesnakes to bite them and still live; and with hundreds of other tales of mysterious happenings and healings.

Moreover, I have made myself familiar with the lives of great men and women of history and have met and interviewed many outstanding men and women in all lines of human endeavor. Often I have wondered just what it was that took them to the top. I have seen coaches take seemingly inferior baseball and football teams and infuse them with something that caused them to win. In the Depression days, I saw badly whipped sales organizations do an abrupt about-face and bring in more business than ever before.

Apparently I was born with a huge bump of curiosity, for 1 have always had an insatiable yearning to seek answers and explanations. This quest has taken me to many strange places, brought to light many peculiar cases, and caused me to read every book I could get my hands on dealing with religions, cults, and physical and mental sciences. I have read literally thousands of books on modem psychology, metaphysics, ancient magic, Voodoo, Yoga,

Theosophy, Christian Science, Unity, Truth, New Thought, Couéism, and many others dealing with what I call "Mind Stuff," as well as the philosophies and teachings of great masters of the past.

Many were nonsensical, others strange, and many very profound. Gradually I discovered that a golden thread runs through all the teachings and makes them work for those who sincerely accept and apply them, and that thread can be named in the single word *belief.* It is this same element or factor -- belief -- that causes people to be cured through mental healing, enables others to climb high the ladder of success, and gets phenomenal results for all who accept it. *Why* belief works miracles is something that cannot be satisfactorily explained; but have no doubt that there's genuine magic in believing. "The magic of believing" became a phrase around which my thoughts steadily revolved.

I am convinced that the so-called secret fraternal organizations guard a real "royal secret" which very few members ever grasp. The conclusion must be that "no mind ever receives the truth until it is prepared to receive it." One order provides candidates with a very profound book (to be studied in connection with the degree work), which itself would be practically an open-sesame to life if the candidates could understand and follow its tenets. But few read it, complaining that "it is too deep" for them. I am convinced, too, that some of these organizations, like many secret orders which possess a knowledge and understanding of life, use parables and misinterpretations to mislead.

When *T.N.T. -- It Rocks the Earth* was first published, I imagined that it would be easily understood since I had written it simply. But as the years went by, some readers protested that it was too much in digest form. Others said they couldn't understand it. I had assumed that most people knew something about the power of thought. Now I realize that I was mistaken, and those who had an understanding of the subject were comparatively few. Later, over many years of lecturing before clubs, business and sales organizations, I discovered that most people were vitally interested in the subject, but that it had to be fully explained. Finally, I undertook to write this book *[The Magic of Believing]* in words that anyone can understand -- and with the hope that it will help many to reach their goals in life.

The science of thought is as old as man himself. The wise men of all ages have known it and used it. The only thing I have done is to put the subject in modern language and bring to the reader's attention what some of today's outstanding minds are doing to substantiate the great truths that have come down through the centuries.

Fortunately for the world, people are coming to the realization that there is something to this "mind-stuff" after all. I believe that millions of people would like to get a better understanding of it -- and prove that it *does* work.

Therefore, let me start by relating a few experiences from my own life, with the hope that they will give you a better understanding of the entire science.

Early in 1918, I landed in France as a "casual" soldier, unattached to a regular company. As a result, it was several weeks before my service record (necessary for my pay) caught up with me. During that period I had no money to buy gum, candy, cigarettes, and the like, since the few dollars I had before sailing had been spent at the transport ship's canteen to relieve the monotony of the regular menu. Every time I saw a man light a cigarette or chew a stick of gum, it reminded me that I was without money to spend on myself. Certainly, I was eating, and the army clothed me and provided me with a place on the ground to sleep, but I grew bitter at having no spending money and no way of getting any. One night en-route to the forward area on a crowded troop train when sleep was out of the question, I made up my mind that on my return to civilian life, I would have a *lot* of money. The whole pattern of my life was altered at that moment.

True, I had been something of a reader in my youth; the Bible had been a must in our family. As a boy I was interested in wireless telegraphy, X-rays, high-frequency apparatus, and similar manifestations of electricity, and I had read every book on these subjects I could find. But while I was familiar with such terms as radiation frequencies, vibrations, oscillations, magnetic influences, etc., in those days they meant nothing to me outside of the strictly electrical field. Perhaps my first inkling of a connection between the mind and electrical or vibratory influences came when upon my completing law school, an instructor gave me an old book, Thomson Jay Hudson's *Law of Psychic Phenomena.* I read it, but only superficially. Either I did not understand it, or my mind was not ready to receive its profound truths. On that fateful night in the spring of 1918, when I told myself that some day I would have a lot of money, I did not realize that I was laying the groundwork for a series of causes which would unleash forces that would bring accomplishment. As a matter of fact, the idea never entered my mind that I could develop a fortune with my thinking and believing.

My Army classification card listed me as a newspaper man. I had been attending an Army Training School to qualify for a commission, but the whole training-school program was discontinued just as we finished the course; thus most of us landed in France as enlisted men. However, I considered myself a qualified journalist and felt that there was a better place for me in the American Expeditionary Force. Yet like many others, I found myself pushing wheelbarrows and lugging heavy shells and other ammunition.

Then one night at an ammunition depot near Toul, things began to happen. I was ordered to appear before the Commanding Officer, who asked me whom I knew at First Army Headquarters. I didn't know a soul there and didn't even know where it was located, and I told him so. Then he showed me orders directing me to report there immediately. A car and driver were provided, and the next morning found me at First Army Headquarters in charge of a daily progress bulletin. I was answerable only to a colonel.

During the months that followed, I frequently thought about the commission to which I was entitled. Then the links began to form into a chain. One day, entirely out of a clear sky, came orders transferring me to the *Stars and Stripes,* the Army newspaper; I had long had an ambition to be on its staff, but had done nothing about it. The next day, as I was preparing to leave for Paris, I was called before the colonel who showed me a telegram signed by the Adjutant General's office at GHQ, asking if I was available for commission. The colonel asked whether I would rather have a commission than report to the Army newspaper. Foreseeing that the war would soon end and I would be happier among other newspaper men, I said I would prefer the transfer to the *Stars and Stripes.* I never learned who was responsible for the telegram, but obviously something was working in my behalf.

Following the armistice, my desire to get out of the Army became insistent. I wanted to begin building that fortune. But the *Stars and Stripes* did not suspend publication until the summer of 1919, and it was August before I got home. However, the forces I had unconsciously set in motion were already setting the stage for me.

About nine-thirty the next morning after my arrival home, I received a telephone call from the president of a club in which I had been active. He told me to call a prominent man in the investment banking business who had read about my return and had expressed a wish to see me before I resumed newspaper work. I called the man and, two days later, embarked upon a long career as an investment banker, which later led me to the vice-presidency of a well-known Pacific Coast firm.

While my salary was smart at the start, I realized that I was in a business where there were many opportunities to **make money**. Just how I was to make it was then not revealed, but I just knew that I would have that fortune I had in mind. In less than ten years, I did have it, and not only was it sizable, but I was a substantial stockholder in the company and had several outside profitable interests. During those years I had constantly before me a mental picture of wealth.

Many people in moments of abstraction or while talking on the telephone engage in doodling -- drawing or sketching odd designs and patterns upon paper. My doodling was in the form of dollar signs like these -- $$$$$ -- $$$ -- $$ -- $$$$ -- on every paper that came across my desk. The cardboard covers of all the files placed before me daily were scrawled with these markings, as were the covers of telephone directories, scratch-pads, and even the face of important correspondence. I want my readers to remember this detail, because it suggests the mechanics to be used in applying this magic which I'll explain in detail later.

During the past years, I have found that by far the greatest problems bothering most people are financial ones.

With today's intense competition, millions are facing the same kinds of problems. However, it matters little to what ends this science is used. It will be effective in achieving the object of your desire -- and in this connection, let me tell another experience.

Shortly after the idea of *T.N.T. -- It Rocks the Earth* came to me but before I put it on paper, I took a trip to the Orient and sailed on the *Empress of Japan,* noted for its excellent cuisine. In my travels through Canada and in Europe I had developed a fondness for Trappist cheese made by the Trappist monks of Quebec. When I couldn't find it on the ship's menu, I laughingly complained to the chief steward that I had sailed on his ship only to get some of the famous "Trappist" cheese. He replied that he was sorry, but there was none aboard.

The more I thought about it, the more I hungered for some of that cheese. One night a ship's party was held. Upon returning to my cabin quarters after midnight, I found a big table had been set up in one of the rooms. On it was the largest cheese I had ever seen. It was "Trappist" cheese.

Later I asked the chief steward where he found it. "I was certain we had none aboard when you first mentioned it," he answered, "but you seemed so set on having some, I made up my mind to search through all the ship's stores. We found it in the emergency storeroom in the bottom of the hold." Something was working for me on that trip, too, for I had no claim to **anything but ordinary** service. However, I sat at the executive officer's table and was frequently his personal guest in his quarters, as well as on inspection trips through the ship.

Naturally the treatment I received made a great impression on me, and in Honolulu, I often thought how nice it would be to receive comparable attention on my journey home on another ship. One afternoon I got the sudden impulse to leave for the mainland. It was about closing time when I appeared at the ticket agency to ask what reservations I could get. A ship was leaving the next day at noon, and I purchased the only remaining cabin ticket.

The next day, just a few minutes before noon, as I started up the gangplank, I said to myself in an offhand manner, "They treated you as a king on the *Empress of Japan.* The least you can do here is to sit at the captain's table. Sure, you'll sit at the captain's table."

The ship got under way. As we steamed out of the harbor, the dining-room steward asked passengers to appear in the dining room for assignment to tables. When I came before him, about half the assignments had been made. He asked for my ticket, glanced at it and then at me, saying, "Oh yes, table A, seat No. 5." It was the captain's table, and I was seated directly across from him. Aboard that ship, many things happened which pertain to the subject of this book, the most prominent being a party supposed to be in honor of my birthday -- just an idea of the captain's, because my birthday was actually months away.

Later, when I found myself lecturing, I thought it would be wise to get a letter from the captain substantiating the story and I wrote him. He replied, "Sometimes as we go through life, instinctively we get the idea to do this or that. That noon I was sitting in the doorway of my cabin watching the passengers come up the gangplank, and as you came aboard, something told me to seat you at my table. Beyond that I cannot explain, any more than I can explain how I can frequently stop my ship at the right spot at the pier at the first try."

People who have heard the story -- and who know nothing about the magic of believing -- have declared that it was mere coincidence that the captain selected me. I am positive it wasn't, and I'm also certain that this captain (who knows quite a bit about this science) will agree with me. Aboard that ship were dozens of people far more important than I could ever be. I carried nothing to set me apart, being one of those who can pass in a crowd. So obviously it wasn't the clothes I wore or the way I looked that prompted the captain to pick me out of several hundred passengers to receive personal attention.

In presenting to you this very workable science, I am aware that the subject has been handled before from many angles, but also realize that many people shy away from any approach that smacks of religion, the occult, or the metaphysical. Accordingly, I am using the language of a business-man who believes that sincere thinking, dear writing, and simple language Will get any message across.

You have often heard it said that you can if you believe you can. An old Latin proverb says, "Believe that you have it, and you have it." Belief is the motivating force that enables you to achieve your goal. If you are ill and imbedded deeply within you is the thought or belief that you will recover, the odds are that you will. It's the belief or the basic confidence within you that brings outward material results. I speak of normal and mentally healthy people. I wouldn't tell a handicapped person that he could excel in baseball or football. Nor would I tell a woman who was quite plain-looking that she could make herself into a great beauty overnight, since the odds are against it. Yet these things *could* happen, for there have been many remarkable cures. And when more is learned about the powers of the mind, I firmly believe that we shall witness many cures that today's **medical profession** deems impossible. Finally, I would never discourage anyone; for in this life, anything can happen -- and what can help bring it to pass is Hope.

Dr. Alexander Cannon was a distinguished British scientist and physician whose books on the general subject of thought stirred up controversy here and abroad. He declared that while today a man cannot grow a new leg (as a crab can grow a new claw), he could if the mind of man hadn't rejected the possibility. The eminent scientist claimed that if the thought is changed in the innermost depths of the unconscious mind, then man will grow a new leg as easily as the crab grows a new claw. I know, such a statement may sound incredible, but how do we know that it will not be done some day?

Frequently I lunch with a group of medical men, all specialists in various branches of medicine and surgery. I know that if I voiced such an idea, they would suggest that I have my head examined. However, I find that some of these doctors, especially those more recently graduated from our better schools, are no longer dosing their minds to the role that thought plays in causing and curing functional disturbances in the body.

A few weeks before I wrote this chapter, a neighbor came to me to explain how his warts happened to disappear. During a stay at the hospital, he had wandered out on the porch where another convalescent patient was conversing with a friend. Said the visitor to the other patient, "So you would like to get rid of the warts on your hand? Well, just let me count them, and they'll disappear."

My neighbor said he looked at the stranger for a moment, then said: "While you're about it, will you count mine, too?" He did, and my neighbor thought no more about it until after he had gone home and he happened to look at his hands one day. "The mess of warts had entirely disappeared!" he told me.

I told this story to a group of doctors one day. A well-known specialist -- and personal friend -- grunted, saying, "Preposterous!" Across the table, another **doctor** who had recently been teaching in a **medical school** came to my aid, declaring that there were many authenticated cases of suggestion having been used to cure warts.

I was tempted to remind them that several years before, newspapers and medical journals had reported how Heim, a Swiss geologist, had removed warts by suggestion, and had also cited the procedure of Professor Block, another Swiss specialist, in his use of psychology and suggestion for the same purpose. Back in January, 1945, Columbia University's College of Physicians and Surgeons set up the first psychoanalytic and psychosomatic clinic in this country for the purpose of studying the relationship between the unconscious mind and the body. I kept silent, feeling that I was too outnumbered for an argument.

Since this conversation, considerable publicity was given to the findings of Dr. Frederick Kalz, a noted Canadian authority who flatly stated that suggestion works in many cases, even to curing warts that are infectious and caused by a virus. In a 1945 article in the *Canadian Medical Association Journal,* Dr. Kalz declared that, "In every country in the world some magic procedures to cure warts are known...It may be anything from covering the wart with spider-webs to burying toad eggs on a crossroad at new moon; all these magic procedures are effective, if the patient *believes in them."* In describing the treatment of patients with skin trouble, he says, "I have often prescribed the very same ointment, accompanied by some promising words, which has been tried unsuccessfully by some other medical man, and got credit for a quick cure." He also points out that X-ray therapy is especially suggestive; it works even when the technician fails to switch on the high power! Experiments with systematic fake irradiation bear out this observation. Here in Dr. Kalz's work we see actual examples of the *magic of believing* at work in the curing of warts and the treatment of skin trouble.

Another time my medical friends and I were discussing telepathy. I remarked that some of our greatest students and scholars believed in it. Dr. **Alexis Carrel**, of the Rockefeller Institute for Medical Research, was not only a thorough believer in the phenomenon but declared that there was definite scientific proof that man could project his thought even at great distances into other minds.

"Oh, he was just a senile old man," remarked another specialist at the table, a nationally known member of the American Medical Association.

I looked at him with astonishment, for Dr. Carrel won the Nobel Prize for iris medical research. When he put forth his ideas in that remarkable book, *Man the Unknown,* published in 1935, he was regarded as one of the world's foremost medical scientists and investigators.

I have no quarrel with the medical fraternity. Quite the contrary, for its members are generally sincere, able, and open-minded men, and a number are among my closest friends. However, some medical specialists, especially those inclined to restrict their studies to their respective fields, refuse to accept anything that may upset their early teachings and dogmatic beliefs. This resistance is not confined to the **medical profession**: countless specialists in other lines, including business, know very little outside of their chosen fields, and their minds are closed to any idea beyond their limited imaginations. Frequently, I have offered to lend books to these various specialists -- only to be told, after informing them of the contents, that they were not interested.

Paradoxically, many apparently well-educated men and women, successful in their respective fields, will, in their broad ignorance, condemn the idea of thought power and make no endeavor to learn more about it -- *yet every one of them has unconsciously made use of it!* Again, many people will believe only what they like to believe or what fits into their own scheme of things, summarily rejecting anything to the contrary.

Countless men whose ideas developed the very civilization we live in have been hooted at, slandered, even crucified by the ignoramuses of their times. I think of the words of Marie Corelli, the English novelist who became world famous in the 19th century:

The very idea that any one creature (human) should be fortunate enough to secure some particular advantage which others, through their own indolence or indifference, have missed is sufficient to excite the envy of the weak or the anger of the ignorant...It is impossible that an outsider should enter into a clear understanding of the mystical spiritual-nature world around him, and it follows that the teachings and tenets of that spiritual-nature world must be more or less a closed book to such a one-a book, moreover, which he seldom cares or dares to try and open. For this reason, the sages concealed much of their profound knowledge from the multitude, bemuse they rightly recognized the limitations of narrow minds and prejudiced opinions...What the fool cannot learn, he laughs at, thinking that by his laughter he shows superiority instead of latent idiocy.

Great investigators and thinkers of the world, including many famous scientists, are in the open today, freely discussing the subject and giving the results of their experiments. Shortly before his death, Charles P. Steinmetz, famous engineer of the General Electric Company, declared, "The most important advance in the next fifty years will be in the realm of the spiritual -- dealing with the spirit -- thought." Dr. Robert Gault, while professor of Psychology at Northwestern University, was credited with the statement: "We are at the threshold of our knowledge of the latent psychic powers of man."

Much has been written and said about mystical powers, unknown forces, the occult, metaphysics (beyond science), mental physics, psychology (the science of mind), black and white magic, and many kindred subjects, causing most people to believe that they are in the field of the supernatural. Perhaps they are for some. But to me, the only inexplicable thing about these powers is that belief makes them work.

During the years that I have appeared before luncheon clubs, business concerns, and sales organizations, as well as talking over the radio to thousands of people about this science, I have seen results that can be termed phenomenal.

As I said before, many have used it in their business to double, treble, even quadruple their incomes. My files are filled with letters from people in all walks of life, testifying what they have accomplished by using the science. As an instance, I think of Ashley C. Dixon, whose name was once known to thousands of radio listeners in the Pacific Northwest. A number of years ago, he wrote me voluntarily to say that he had studied this subject in an academic way, but had never fully believed it until he was forty-three, when he had only $65 to his name, no employment, and no jobs available. He set out to prove to himself that the science would work. I quote the following excerpts from Mr. Dixon's letter:

"Your book *T.N.T.* put forth in workable form all that I had known before. It was like seeing Niagara Falls for the first time. One knew there was such a place; but confirmation was the actual personal contact with it. And so, *T.N.T.* gave me in print the facts I had known and used, but in a clear form. Here was something I could read and use day by day, holding the thoughts till they were fully demonstrated.

"What has all this been worth to me in dollars and cents? That, of course, is the question of the average man. He wants to see something...in the profit column; something material in the way of dollars and cents. Here's the answer. I have made a hundred thousand dollars, most of it in paid-up insurance and annuities. I have sold my business which costs me $5,000 (originally borrowed) for $30,000, and am now working on a contract to run for the next ten years which will net me $50,000 if I loaf; and more if I care to work. This is not a boast. It is a factual statement of what has actually happened in the past ten years...It cannot be done in a moment, or a day or a month, but it can be done."

In 1934, during the lowest point of the Depression, the head of the Better Business Bureau in a large Pacific Coast city heard of what was happening to firms and individuals who were following my teachings. He decided to investigate my work. Later he congratulated me publicly and subsequently wrote me as follows:

"My statement -- that the teachings have done more to stimulate business here during the past year than any other single factor or agency--is based upon statements by numerous executives who have been using the theme successfully in their businesses...When I first heard of the phenomenal results you were obtaining, I was inclined to question the facts. They seemed too preposterous to be true. But upon investigation, talking with heads of firms using the theme and with salesmen who have doubled and trebled their incomes, as well as hearing many of your lectures and getting into the subject for myself, the terrific and dynamic force embraced by it all becomes apparent. It isn't going to be understood by everyone in a minute, but firms and individuals that accept what you have to give and follow through can expect some startling and extraordinary results. You have fully demonstrated that, and therefore are to be congratulated."

This man has since risen to great heights in the business world and has written me of having seen other practical demonstrations of the workings of this science.

When I started this book, I decided to check with some of the individuals and firms who had written me to certify the phenomenal results they had achieved by using this science. Without exception, every one testified to the continuing progress he had made. One of the most outstanding accounts was related by Mr. Dorr Quayle, once well-known to the Disabled American War Veterans, who was long active in veterans' affairs in the Northwest. In 1937, he wrote me:

"It was no easy matter, at first, to completely accept your ideas. But my circumstances and physical condition forced me to keep at it continuously until understanding came....You see, in February, 1924, I was stricken with partial paralysis of my lower limbs. I needed crutches to even get about at all, and at best, for only short distances, and at a snail's pace. For [a bank executive] who had been active in the business world this forced inactivity was not easy to get used to. It was bearable only because I received government compensation -- my disability being considered due to service during the World War. However, in 1933, the Government dropped me from the compensation rolls, and I was forced to make a living. My home and other properties were about to be repossessed. It was not a pleasant picture, nor a hopeful future.

"Necessity forced me to put into practice the principles you explained so well. Sticking to it proves them. Possibly I was favored because I couldn't quit the insurance and public accounting business -- due to my inability to enter any other kind of work. But persistence gives confidence, and continued fight mental attitude followed by consistent action will bring success. I haven't reached the degree of success I desire, but that does not bother me at all, for now I am making a good living, have saved my properties, and know the formula that leads to the fullest success. When you have that knowing *inside* you, fear vanishes, as do the obstructions to a continued life of all good."

I first met Mr. Quayle just after he had started his business with one desk in the front of a plumbing shop. In the following years, it was a pleasure to see him move from place to place, his business growing by leaps and bounds, until he occupied the entire ground floor of a building on one of the main thoroughfares of a great western city. Realizing that his story of achievement was a remarkable one, I asked permission to quote his earlier letter.

"By all means, do so," he replied, "if you think it will help others. You might add that I now have the whole quarters at 20th and Sandy and I employ twenty-two people. I have just brought the business lot between 28th and 29th on Sandy where I shall build my own office building. I sincerely wish that all people would accept your teachings."

At the time I grasped this science, I had no idea that I was later to put it into book form. My primary thought was to use it to save my own organization from bankruptcy. I was then vice-president of an investment banking firm, and we had been caught in the economic crisis and were headed for disaster.

I don't know whether I was inspired, but I dictated the first draft of my brochure in its entirety in less than five hours, without notes or references of any kind before me. At the same time the idea for the brochure came to me, the words, "cosmic consciousness," floated before my mind. They meant nothing then.

But after *T.N.T. -- It Rocks the Earth* was published, it reached a woman author living in New York, who wrote me as follows:

"Seriously, I've been eating and sleeping [your] philosophy for the last ten years. It brought me to New York on no carfare; it sold my stuff to publishers when I had a lousy little job earning $30 a week...It took me to Europe a couple of times, and bought me silver foxes."

In the same letter, she urged me to read Dr. Richard Maurice Bucke's *Cosmic Consciousness,* declaring that it contained brilliant accounts of the actual experience of illumination. When I did, I was astounded to discover that my experience actually paralleled the illuminations listed and explained by Dr. Bucke. In the original draft of my brochure, I had described in detail my experience with "brilliant white light." But subsequently, when I showed the manuscript to a close friend, he urged me to tone down the wording: "People won't know what you are talking about in referring to that 'white light' -- some may think you've gone off the deep end." Consequently, I changed it. But those of you know something about "cosmic illumination" and have read my earlier small book will catch my reference to the "light." However, the memory of that singular experience will always remain with me: in those few seconds, I received more knowledge and understanding than I had ever received in years of reading and studying.

In the same period, it came to me in a flash why my firm was going on the rocks -- not because of the threatening outside happenings and events, but because of the mental attitude of our employees. We were all succumbing to mass fear-thoughts: we feared that the Depression was weakening our spirit and sweeping *everything* downhill to financial disaster. With our own thoughts of ruin, we were attracting the disaster to ourselves.

It occurred to me that to save the firm and to begin fighting the Depression itself, all I needed to do was reverse the thinking of every person connected with our organization. I set about doing that very thing. As Frank W. Camp, who wrote the introduction to my brochure declared, it was followed "by the most remarkable transformation of individuals and organization as well."

I admit that some of my statements may be ridiculed by classroom psychologists. But every day, thousands of people demonstrate for themselves that the science works. As for you, the reader, the main point to consider is whether it will work for you. The only way you can find out is to *try it yourself.*

I give you this science, in the confident knowledge that no matter how you use it, you will get results. But I do wish to repeat a warning given in my brochure: *Never use it for harmful or evil purposes.*

Since the beginning, there have been two great subtle forces in the world -- good and evil. Both are terrifically powerful in their respective scopes and cycles. The basic principle operating both is *mind power* -- massed mind power. Sometimes evil appears to have the upper hand, and at other times good is at the controls. It is mind power that has built empires, and we have seen how it can be used to destroy them -- history has recorded the facts.

If you read this book reflectively, you will understand how the science can be used with terribly destructive force, as well as for good and constructive results. It is like many natural forces, such as water and fire, which are among men's greatest benefactors. Yet both can be hideously catastrophic, depending upon whether they are used for constructive or destructive purposes.

Therefore, take great care that you do not misuse the science of "Mind Stuff." I cannot emphasize this too strongly, for if you employ it for harmful or evil purposes, it will boomerang and destroy you just as it has others down through the centuries. These are not idle words, but solemn words of warning.

* * * * * *

About Bob Choat

I am known as America's #1 Mind-Body Transformation Expert and author of 'Mind Your Own Fitness.'

I consider myself the "average guy" who is on this path of self-discovery. Along the way I decided that I want to make a difference, especially in the areas of health and fitness. It's all about that journey for all of us and I'm no different.

As the son of a career soldier and a Japanese mother, I've had the advantage of traveling the world as a child and living in many different areas. While I don't have what anyone would consider 'roots" to any one area, I do look at myself as lucky. Learning about different cultures, even within the United States, has expanded my perception.

From early on in my life I was exposed to the healthy side of life as well as the unhealthy side. My father was a life-long smoker and lived his life unhealthy. I remember him saying how much he hated to eat spinach as well as many other veggies. It was no wonder that he suffered from many cardiovascular diseases which led to his passing in 1983 under the age of 50.

Just as I was lucky in being exposed to many cultures, I was also lucky to see both sides of health. My Japanese uncle, Keiji, represents what one could be like when living a healthy lifestyle. Even into his late 90s he showed vibrancy. Seeing so many sides of life led me to look at my own. I did manage to serve in the Marines and the Los Angeles Police Department. I love action and fitness was part of repertoire in both lines of work.

I've made my fair share of mistakes. Even in health and fitness. Like I said earlier, I'm like the average guy. Yet, I went on a quest to want to learn more, especially in the area of how we think and believe. My question became, "What is that driving factor that leads us to do what we do?"

I will never forget my father coming up to me back in high school and saying, "Son, I know you're into sports and exercising. That will all change by the time you get into your 30's. You're not going to do any of that, your life will change." That was his mindset regarding health and fitness. He stopped exercising and didn't really believe in it. At the age of 39 he had his first heart attack. And just under 10 years later he passed away from the complications of a stroke.

His attitude about health is much the same I've witnessed in many parts of the United States. Since the 1970s I've seen many changes to the health of the average person (which is the one area where I am different). I wanted to answer the question I thought about above. So began my journey into learning.

From graduate level studies in psychology to courses in personal training, I absorbed it all. The practical application of hypnosis I learned at Hypnosis Motivation Institute in Tarzana, CA helped quite a bit in knowing how to change the mindset of people.

Earlier, as a direct response copywriter, I learned how certain words can have an influence. My studies in psychology via the academic route helped, though it was the study outside of it is where I really learned. Traditional universities do not teach methods like Cognitive Behavioral Therapy (CBT) and Rational Emotive Behavioral Therapy (REBT). So I decided that I wanted to learn more, beyond the university walls.

I took courses in REBT as well as EEG Neurofeedback. I was able to combine all of this with trainings in fitness as well. I received my certification in personal training from the National Academy of Sports Medicine. While working on my dissertation I learned about epigenetics and how our lifestyle affects the expression of our genes. I also studied extensively in neuroscience and became a member of the Cognitive Neuroscience Society.

I could go on and on about this credential and that credential. It's not going to do you a bit of good, except I do my homework in what works and what doesn't work. While I educate my clients and others in how to change their mental state towards fitness, I also live by example.

In June 2012 I set my all-time best in non-stop pull-ups by doing 57. My best in the Marines was 44 pull-ups. I also did over 1000 push-ups in 30 minutes in June 2012. In recent years I received my 5th degree black-belt in Kenpo Karate and the same in American Modern Jujitsu as well as becoming a Senior Instructor in Jeet Kune Do. There's more in that arena too.

I'm a big believer in moving forward and not resting on past laurels. I will keep challenging myself to perform at my best as much as possible. I can't tell you to do the same thing if I am not doing it either. So, keep challenging your mind and body to get and stay healthy and fit and I will do the same.

Contact Information

Websites:

bobchoat.com

optimallifeseminars.com

weightlosstransformationstation.com

Email: **bobchoat@gmail.com**

Facebook.com/coachbobchoat

Twitter.com/BobChoat

LinkedIn.com/in/bobchoat

Pinterest.com/bobchoat

Printed in Great Britain
by Amazon